WORLD'S
DEADLIEST
ANIMALS

DEADLIEST

DEADLIEST
DEADLIEST
DEAD

WORLD'S
DEADLIEST
DEADLIEST
ANIMALS

DEADLIEST
DEADLIEST
DEAD

WORLD'S
DEADLIEST
DEADLIEST
ANIMALS

LD'S
DEADLIEST
DEADLIEST
DEAD
ANIMALS

ST
DEADLIEST
DEADLIEST

WORLD'S
DEADLIEST
DEAD
ANIMALS

ST
DEADLIEST
DEADLIEST

WORLD'S DEADLIEST ANIMALS

Summersdale Publishers Ltd
46 West Street
Chichester
West Sussex
PO19 1RP
UK

www.summersdale.com

Printed and bound in China

ISBN: 978-1-84953-303-4

Substantial discounts on bulk quantities of Summersdale books are available to corporations, professional associations and other organisations. For details contact Summersdale Publishers by telephone: +44 (0) 1243 771107, fax: +44 (0) 1243 786300 or email: nicky@summersdale.com.

WORLD'S DEADLIEST ANIMALS

MATT ROPER

summersdale

ABOUT THE AUTHOR

Matt Roper is a writer and journalist living in Brazil. A former feature writer and correspondent for the *Daily Mirror*, he lived in London for eight years before moving to Brazil, where he now contributes regularly to all the UK's national newspapers. He has written four other books: *101 Crazy Ways to Die*, *World's Weirdest Sports*, *World's Weirdest Obsessions* and *World's Weirdest Animals.*

CONTENTS

INTRODUCTION

It's a cruel, cruel world.

All we want is a bit of peace, love and harmony on Earth, but what are the chances of that when even Mother Nature appears to have a sadistic streak?

Innocently set foot where a harmless-looking frog has just hopped and you might find yourself with deadly venom in your system; gently pat a pretty little songbird and you could end up choking to death as a potent toxin causes your oesophagus to close up. And don't even think about saying boo to a moose – you'll get a hoof kick that'll rupture your insides.

If you thought there was nothing worse than man's inhumanity to man, then you've never seen a frenzied cassowary bird disembowel someone with a single kick, an angry sloth bear rip a person's face right off or a great white shark devour a diver piece by piece with its killer jaws.

This book collects together some of the animals considered most deadly to man, giving descriptions of their lethal nature and gruesome details on how long you have left and the last thing you'll feel if you're unlucky enough to encounter them.

It just goes to show that we humans aren't as in control of this world as we'd like to believe. Turn the page to find out about the deadly animals that really call the shots...

GOLDEN DART FROG

Phyllobates terribilis
LIVES Colombia's Pacific Coast
EATS Beetles, other small insects

It doesn't grow any bigger than 5 cm in length, but what the golden dart frog lacks in size it more than makes up for in pure, unadulterated deadliness.

Considered the most poisonous creature on Earth, its back oozes a slimy neurotoxin which is scarily toxic: humans have been known to have died just by touching the bright yellow frog's skin, by drinking water it has swum in, or even by walking barefoot across a surface it has happened to hop over.

And no wonder – just two tenths of a single microgram of its venom can be fatal once in a human's bloodstream, and the golden dart can exude up to 200 micrograms. Or, put another way, this frog is capable of killing 1,000 humans – a yellow, hopping weapon of mass destruction.

TIME YOU'VE GOT LEFT: Less than a minute

THE LAST THING YOU'LL FEEL: Once absorbed through the skin into your bloodstream, the frog's toxin travels straight to your heart where it attacks the nerves, making breathing impossible. You won't feel much after that. Stressed asphyxiation leads to coma, cardiac arrest, then death.

WANDERING SPIDER

Ctenidae (family)
LIVES Central and South America
EATS Crickets, lizards, mice

Emergency room staff in Brazil can spot a patient who has been bitten by a wandering spider, because its powerful venom has a peculiar side effect – it leaves male victims with a painful erection which can last for hours.

These, though, are the lucky ones, who have felt the huge fangs of the world's deadliest spider sink into their flesh and lived to tell the tale. This aggressive, easily angered arachnid bites and kills more people than any other spider, charging and even pouncing on its victims to deliver its deadly bite.

The eight-legged, eight-eyed creature gets its name because it wanders around on the ground, rather than residing in a lair or having a web. During the day it usually searches for cover in people's homes, hiding in dark places like boxes, wardrobes, clothes baskets or inside discarded shoes, which is one of the reasons why so many people experience a deadly encounter.

TIME YOU'VE GOT LEFT: 30 minutes
THE LAST THING YOU'LL FEEL: After the excruciating pain comes swelling, cold sweats, heart palpitations, loss of muscle control, asphyxiation, then death.

HYENA

Hyaenidae (family)
LIVES Africa, Asia and the Middle East
EATS Goats, chickens, other animals

Most big cats at least have the decency to make sure you're dead before they start feeding on your flesh, but not their distant relative, the hyena, which will get stuck in just as soon as it's able to rip you open – and will normally start on the intestines.

Although it will kill smaller prey by violently shaking them and breaking their spine, the hyena lacks any efficient weapon to deal with larger prey, so it will usually start eating as soon as its victim is brought down.

It's not uncommon for a large animal to still be alive when the hyena clan is already munching on its insides – and the same goes for humans, dozens of which are killed by this savannah scavenger every year. Often victims are pounced upon while they are sleeping outside at night, waking up to find themselves in a gory horror movie as a pack of voracious predators rips out their entrails.

TIME YOU'VE GOT LEFT: 2 minutes
THE LAST THING YOU'LL FEEL: Being ripped open and disembowelled while you're still conscious can't be a pleasant experience. Thankfully, it won't last long as the shock or blood loss will quickly bring blackout and death.

AFRICANISED BEE

Apis mellifera

LIVES South America and southern USA

EATS Pollen, nectar

Like something out of an apocalyptic thriller, the Africanised bee is a man-made mutant that was created by scientists in a lab.

Now known as 'killer' bees, the insects are descended from 26 Tanzanian queen bees that a Brazilian biologist had interbred to try to create a strain better adapted to tropical conditions. Instead of making more productive breeds, however, he ended up with a strain of insanely territorial, mindlessly aggressive bees which attack in swarms and sting their victims thousands of times. And just when he realised he'd created a monster, a replacement bee keeper accidentally released them from his farm near São Paulo, south-east Brazil, in 1957.

To date, the bees have killed over 1,000 people in South and Central America, and colonies have been found as far north as Texas.

TIME YOU'VE GOT LEFT: 30 minutes

THE LAST THING YOU'LL FEEL: The sting of the Africanised bee is no more painful than any other bee; the difference is you won't get stung once or twice, but by a swarm of thousands. That's enough to cause fever, vomiting, headaches, convulsions and death.

MOOSE

Alces alces
LIVES Northern USA, Canada and northern Europe
EATS Plants, fruit

In Canada, where its population exceeds 100,000, the moose is responsible for more human deaths than any other animal, even the fearsome grizzly bear. In fact, the moose is heavier than a bear, weighing in at more than 100 stone, and can run at speeds of up to 40 mph – not to mention the set of spiky antlers splaying 6 ft from end to end. Pretty impressive for a creature whose name means 'eater of twigs'.

Particularly aggressive when defending a calf, the humongous beast will charge without warning or provocation. The official advice if you find yourself being stomped on by 100 stone of angry moose is to curl up into a foetal position and do nothing – trying to beat it off will only cause it to keep kicking.

TIME YOU'VE GOT LEFT: 10 minutes
THE LAST THING YOU'LL FEEL: The moose attacks by first kicking forward then trampling with its sharp hooves which, when followed by 100 stone of body, will rupture your insides and cause massive internal bleeding. Without immediate medical attention, this will result in death by blood loss.

SIAFU ANT

Formicidae (family)
LIVES East Africa
EATS Small animals

It might be tiny, slow and completely blind, but the siafu ant, when found in large numbers, can reduce a human being to a pile of bones in a matter of hours.

Also known as the 'army' or 'driver' ant, the extremely carnivorous critter is the only insect known to attack and devour people and, according to locals, can smell human flesh more than a mile away. The ant, which has very large, sharp jaws and a venomous sting, sets out in search of food in columns that can consist of as many as 50 million individuals – complete with sentries that set up a perimeter to protect the smaller members of the colony – devouring everything that stands in its way.

Attacks by siafu ants on babies, the injured and infirm, or people in a deep sleep, have all been reported.

TIME YOU'VE GOT LEFT: 12 hours

THE LAST THING YOU'LL FEEL: After the large ants have dug into your skin with their strong jaws, the small ants will get under the skin and begin eating your flesh. During the attack they will attempt to go into any opening they can find, including your mouth and nose, and you will eventually die of asphyxia after the ants crawl into your lungs.

BOX JELLYFISH

Cubozoa (class)

LIVES Waters around Asia and Australia

EATS Shrimps, plankton, other jellyfish

One of the animal kingdom's most prolific mass murderers, the box jellyfish has caused at least 5,567 recorded deaths since 1954, and counting.

Its venom is also among the most deadly in the world, attacking the heart, nervous system and skin cells all at once, and so overpoweringly painful that many victims die before even reaching shore. Those who have been stung and survived have needed up to 40 mg of morphine to ease the pain – a broken leg requires just 4 mg.

Also known as the sea wasp, the jellyfish has developed into a sophisticated killing machine, with four brains, 24 eyes, and 60 toxic tentacles that stretch up to 2 m long and are covered in four billion venomous fibres.

TIME YOU'VE GOT LEFT: 3 minutes

THE LAST THING YOU'LL FEEL: The pain as the nematocysts (barbed, venomous cells) on the tentacles dig into your flesh is indescribable. The venom will immediately start killing and digesting your skin, turning the tissue into a black soup, although you probably won't notice that as you go from convulsions to cardiac arrest, coma, then death.

DEADLY ANIMAL FACTS

The stonefish is so-named because it can disguise itself as a rock – until someone steps on it, at which point it injects a deadly venom through the spines on its back. Amazingly, the stonefish can survive out of the water for up to 20 hours at a time.

A scuba diver was reported to have been swallowed whole by a great white shark near Cape Town, South Africa, in June 2005. Shocked witnesses told how the huge shark rose up behind 22-year-old Henri Murray, opened its jaws and gulped the unsuspecting swimmer down.

MARBLED CONE SNAIL

Conus marmoreus
LIVES Indian Ocean, western Pacific Ocean
EATS Fish

It's the kind of pretty little shell you might want to pick up and take home... but if you do, it will probably be the last thing you do.

Despite its unassuming size and captivating, intricately-patterned shell, the marbled cone snail is actually one of the deadliest sea creatures on Earth: one drop of its venom is so powerful it can kill more than 20 men.

The murderous mollusc – which likes to hang around precisely in the shallow, warm waters where unassuming shell pickers might be paddling – shoots out a poison-tipped harpoon at lightning speed from underneath its shell, instantly paralysing its prey. And don't think you can avoid it by standing behind it: the snail can shoot in any direction, even backwards. Oh, and there's no known antidote.

TIME YOU'VE GOT LEFT: 5 minutes
THE LAST THING YOU'LL FEEL: First comes intense, agonising pain – and it's pretty much downhill from there. Swelling, dizziness, numbness and nausea, followed by loss of coordination, disturbed sensory perception, muscle paralysis, then finally respiratory failure.

HIPPOPOTAMUS

Hippopotamus amphibius
LIVES Africa
EATS Fruit, grass, leaves, vegetables

You'd think any animal weighing over 570 stone would barely be able to move, never mind chase a person at speeds of up to 30 mph – but that's why the hippo isn't just any animal.

It's also the reason why this huge beast kills more humans in Africa than any other large animal – along with the fact it has 20-in.-long teeth and the strongest jaw of any land animal, capable of clamping down at 6,000 lb of pressure.

Despite being a herbivore, the hippo aggressively defends its territory, fighting to the death, which with another hippo can take hours, but with a human takes a matter of seconds. When attacking, the lumbering giant, which is most closely related to whales and dolphins, tries to confuse their foe by furiously wagging its tail in front of its anus, spraying poo in all directions.

TIME YOU'VE GOT LEFT: Minutes
THE LAST THING YOU'LL FEEL: Although it could quite easily crush you to death, the hippo prefers to kill by biting down with its huge jaws. Just as an added insult, you'll probably also get a mouthful of poo just before you die.

TAPEWORM

Cestoda (class)

LIVES Worldwide, but rare in Europe and USA

EATS Digested food

There can't be many worse ways to die than getting a worm infestation in your brain caused by a big adult tapeworm wriggling around in your gut.

The tapeworm can grow up to 39 ft (12 m) long, after finding its way into your digestive system as an egg or a larva, ingested by eating raw or improperly cooked meat. It then anchors itself to the intestine wall, absorbing all the body's nutrients for itself – meaning no matter how much you eat, you'll still be malnourished.

If left untreated, a tapeworm infection can lead to death by starvation or vitamin deficiency – and if you think it can't get any worse, the tapeworm larvae can burrow through your intestine wall, enter your bloodstream and swim right up to your brain, causing seizures and other neurological problems.

TIME YOU'VE GOT LEFT: 1–2 years

THE LAST THING YOU'LL FEEL: As the tapeworm grows at the rate of 4 cm a week, you'll begin to have stomach pains, experience nausea, vomiting and diarrhoea, along with weight loss and weakness caused by malnutrition. Once the baby worms make it to your brain you will experience insomnia, dizziness, fits and brain deterioration.

POLAR BEAR

Ursus maritimus
LIVES Northern Arctic
EATS Seals, fish

Cute, cuddly and endangered, it's hard not to feel sorry for the poor polar bear – especially when you see it clinging forlornly to a melting iceberg. See one slap the head clean off an unwary arctic explorer, however, and you're likely to feel something else completely – pure, unadulterated fear.

The polar bear is so big and strong it can rip a 12-in.-thick seal out of a 4-in. hole, and kill just about any animal with a single blow from its paw. Not surprisingly, then, a human who upsets it or just gets in its way doesn't stand a chance – at least 100 people are mauled to death every year.

Yet despite its size and strength, this magnificent bear is in rapid decline as global warming causes ice caps to shrink, with a devastating impact on its habit and food sources. Experts warn that polar bear numbers will reduce by nearly one quarter in the next 20 years, to just 25,000.

TIME YOU'VE GOT LEFT: No time
THE LAST THING YOU'LL FEEL: Not much. With so much power in just one paw, a single blow won't just knock you out, it will knock your head right off.

BLUE-RINGED OCTOPUS

Octopodidae (family)
LIVES Australia's southern shores
EATS Crabs, shrimps

The blue-ringed octopus is actually a shy, retiring creature which spends most of its time hiding away in rock crevices. Upset it, however, and it will turn into a ferocious, blood-thirsty monster, armed with a deadly arsenal of chemical weapons.

Among the dangerous neurotoxins this golf-ball-sized sea mollusc carries around with it is tetrodotoxin, a poison that is 10,000 times more powerful than cyanide and which can kill an adult within minutes – and there's no known antidote.

The venom – which the octopus delivers by either spraying it into the water or injecting it with a painless bite – blocks sodium channels, which disables the muscles, meaning that victims are totally paralysed but remain aware of what's happening right to the end.

TIME YOU'VE GOT LEFT: 3 minutes
THE LAST THING YOU'LL FEEL: Its painless bite may seem harmless at first, but death is just round the corner. The first thing you'll feel is nausea, then you'll go blind, lose your sense of touch, speech and ability to swallow. Within three minutes: paralysis, respiratory arrest and death.

PACU FISH

Characidae (family)
LIVES Papua New Guinea
EATS Er, read on...

In Papua New Guinea, the slightest mention of the pacu strikes terror into the heart of men. Why? Well the clue's in its other name – the 'ball cutter'.

The huge, 40-lb fish, a relative of the piranha, zeroes in on the urine stream of men peeing in the water, then uses a set of human-style molars to tear off their testicles, leaving them to bleed to death. It was such an almost unimaginably horrible fate which befell two fishermen who were standing waist-deep in the Sepik River, in July 2001.

The pacu fish is normally found in the Amazon, where its diet is vegetarian, using its teeth to crack open the tough cases of nuts and seeds. The fish was introduced to Papua New Guinea 15 years ago, and due to a lack of suitable vegetation it started getting a taste for something a bit, well, meatier.

TIME YOU'VE GOT LEFT: 30 minutes

THE LAST THING YOU'LL FEEL: Imagine the most gruesome type of medieval torture, then times it by ten. Thankfully, you'll soon lose consciousness as buckets of blood pour out of your body.

RHINOCEROS

Rhinocerotidae (family)
LIVES Africa and Asia
EATS Leafy plants, branches, shoots

If you see 200 stone of rhinoceros charging in full gallop in your direction, don't take it personally. Its eyesight is so bad it can't even see who you are, and is probably charging you just in case you're another rhino, thinking about charging it.

With a lethal, 3-ft-long horn and a charging speed of up to 40 mph, getting bulldozed is a foregone conclusion. But unlike many dangerous animals which kill for food or just for the fun of it, the rhino – which is a herbivore – attacks more out of fear and panic, because it doesn't know if the blurry object in the distance is a threat or not. They have even been observed charging tree trunks and termite mounds.

Of course, that doesn't help the hundreds of people who are gored or charged to death by rhinos every year.

TIME YOU'VE GOT LEFT: Seconds
THE LAST THING YOU'LL FEEL: You might just feel the rhino horn impaling your skin and rupturing your insides before you're flattened by its weight, which is the equivalent of a car, travelling at the speed of a car.

DEADLY ANIMAL FACTS

Why should you never pee in the Amazon? Because of the tiny candiru fish, which will swim up your urine stream and into your urethra, where it lodges itself by shooting out porcupine-like spikes. It is a pain so unbearable many victims die of shock a long time before getting near a hospital.

The man-eating 'Zambesi' or bull shark patrols not only coastal ocean waters but, alarmingly, the murky shallows of freshwater rivers, bringing it into regular contact with humans. The Brisbane River in Australia alone holds over 500 of these killer sharks, and in the floods of 2011 several bull sharks were spotted cruising down the streets of Goodna in Queensland!

TSETSE FLY

Glossinidae (family)
LIVES Mid-continental Africa
EATS Blood of vertebrate animals

It looks just like your average housefly, but the tsetse is more than just a buzzing nuisance: it's a bloodsucking killer responsible for the horrific deaths of up to 300,000 people a year.

As the fly, which has been around for at least 34 million years, drinks its victims' blood it passes along a tiny parasite, *Trypanosoma brucei*, which causes a terrible and fatal disease called sleeping sickness.

The tsetse's painful bite is the start of a slow and agonising death as the parasite, reproducing wildly in the person's bloodstream, overcomes the body's defences and eventually invades the central nervous system, causing the victim to literally go mad.

TIME YOU'VE GOT LEFT: 9–12 months
THE LAST THING YOU'LL FEEL: As the parasite spreads though your bloodstream, you develop anaemia, glandular disorders, and heart and kidney problems. By the time it reaches your central nervous system, you will begin to display maniacal behaviour, before becoming so weak you can't eat or open your eyes and slipping into a coma before you die.

HOODED PITOHUI

Pitohui dichrous

LIVES Papua New Guinea

EATS Beetles

With its beautiful song and pretty, multicoloured plumage, the hooded pitohui looks like it was put on this earth just to cheer us up. But while the songbird can be safely admired from a distance, give it a stroke and you might be looking at something entirely different: paralysis, cardiac arrest and death.

The pitohui's feathers and skin contain the most powerful natural toxin known to man, the same poison that is found in the famous poison dart frogs. Although not naturally venomous, the birds acquire the toxin through eating their favourite snack, the choresine beetle.

Get pecked or scratched by the pitohui and you will experience stinging, numbness and sneezing. However, for some the poison – which the bird itself has developed an immunity to – can also trigger a serious reaction which can kill in a matter of minutes. Not so pretty after all.

TIME YOU'VE GOT LEFT: 10 minutes

THE LAST THING YOU'LL FEEL: A painful sting, followed by tingling and numbness, difficulty breathing, paralysis, cardiac arrest and death.

AFRICAN LION

Panthera leo
LIVES Sub-Saharan Africa and Asia
EATS Large mammals

We all know we shouldn't get too close a lion – but if you're wandering around in big cat territory you'll never know just how near one might be. Most victims have no idea they're about to become a hungry pride's dinner until they're already being ripped apart.

Although it can reach speeds of up to 50 mph in short bursts, a lion actually has little stamina, so rather than charging or chasing down whichever animal it wants to kill, it will stalk it then ambush it, getting to as close as 10 m before suddenly pouncing. It mostly kills by simply holding on to the prey's muzzle until it suffocates, a technique which is clean and quick. And the same goes for humans, hundreds of which fall victim to the lion's superior hunting skills every year.

TIME YOU'VE GOT LEFT: Seconds
THE LAST THING YOU'LL FEEL: Most animals give up the fight almost as soon as they feel the lion's jaws clamped around their face. Humans, though, generally try to beat the beast off, causing the lion to start biting and ripping, so you'll probably lose most of your face before you take your final breath.

LONOMIA CATERPILLAR

Lonomia obliqua
LIVES Southern Brazil, Venezuela
EATS Plants

Nobody suspected a little caterpillar minding its own business on the branches of a local orchard when, in 1989, residents of a small rural community in southern Brazil started dropping dead – doctors were mystified and people suspected that an assassin was on the loose. The mystery was finally solved with the discovery that the lonomia caterpillar was in fact a deadly killer with a powerful anticoagulant venom.

Now nicknamed the 'assassin caterpillar', over 500 people have already fallen victim to its KGB-like method of killing – lodging one of its hundreds of tiny, detachable venomous spines into the skin of anyone who unknowingly brushes against it, releasing the poison and killing them within hours.

TIME YOU'VE GOT LEFT: 4 hours

THE LAST THING YOU'LL FEEL: Redness and swelling is followed by headache, nausea and vomiting. Internal bleeding starts an hour or so later, and huge haematomas (blood swellings) will appear on your skin and internal organs, causing agony. By then it's only a matter of time before your kidneys fail and your brain drowns in blood.

SLOTH BEAR

Melursus (Ursus) ursinus
LIVES India and Sri Lanka
EATS Termites, ants

For centuries the sloth bear has been persecuted by humans – shot by farmers because it damages crops, hunted for its gall bladder, which is used in medicine in Asia, and captured for a lifetime of cruelty as a circus performer.

And perhaps it is for these reasons that the shaggy-haired bear has developed an intense dislike for humankind. In fact, just the slightest whiff of a person is enough to send the normally docile bear into a murderous frenzy. Being mauled to death by any kind of bear is a particularly horrible way to go, but the sloth bear has been known to use its teeth and incredibly long, sharp claws, to go straight for its victim's face, ripping it right off. It was this fate which befell 36 people in the Indian state of Mysore, when a single sloth bear went on a famous killing spree, leaving 12 dead and the rest horribly disfigured.

TIME YOU'VE GOT LEFT: Seconds
THE LAST THING YOU'LL FEEL: If you're lucky you'll black out with the first blow. Many victims, however, are believed to remain conscious even after their face is ripped off, eventually dying from blood loss a long time after the attack.

ELECTRIC EEL

Electrophorus electricus
LIVES Amazon and Orinoco rivers, South America
EATS Fish, amphibians, small birds, small mammals

Every year, hundreds of people mysteriously disappear while swimming in the Amazon River and many believe this snake-like, supercharged fish is the culprit.

The electric eel – which isn't an eel at all but a type of catfish – has about 6,000 specialised cells, called electrocytes, which create and store electricity like batteries. These cells, which take up 80 per cent of its long body, can produce a charge of about 650 V – enough to light a neon lamp or drive a small motor.

A human who gets zapped by such a bolt while swimming would almost certainly be stunned and drown, if not killed by the electrical discharge itself. It is a fate which is believed to have befallen 17-year-old British schoolboy Aaron Goss, who disappeared while swimming in the Amazon in 2006 while on a trip to Ecuador as part of his Duke of Edinburgh Gold Award.

TIME YOU'VE GOT LEFT: Seconds
THE LAST THING YOU'LL FEEL: British standard mains voltage is 220 V, so imagine sticking a fork in the socket and times it by three. You won't feel very much after that.

ORIENTAL RAT FLEA

Xenopsylla cheopis
LIVES Distributed widely around the world
EATS Dead skin cells, blood

It might only be 2.5 mm long, but this creepy-looking flea is one of history's most terrible mass murderers, responsible for a wave of death which wiped out 25 million people in Europe.

Of all the animals it could choose to live on, the rat flea prefers the sewer rat, from which it can pick up the bacterium that causes bubonic plague, believed to be the cause of the dreaded 'Black Death', which decimated the world's population in the fourteenth century. The flea, which can jump 300 times its own body height, spreads the bacteria by biting an infected rat and then biting a human. Once inside a human the disease is extremely infectious, as it can be spread through coughing, sneezing or any physical contact with the victim.

TIME YOU'VE GOT LEFT: 4 days
THE LAST THING YOU'LL FEEL: Two days after you're infected you'll get gangrene on your toes, fingers, lips and nose. Your skin will begin to decompose, even though you're still alive. If that's not bad enough, blood will begin pouring out your ears and black dots will appear over your entire body, until finally comes delirium, coma and death.

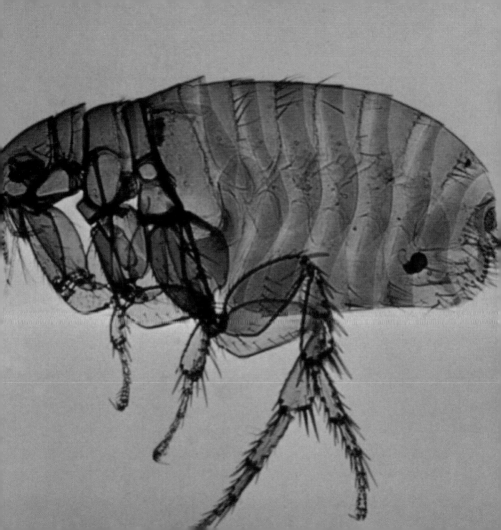

DEADLY
ANIMAL FACTS

The venom of Australia's inland taipan is 400 times more toxic than that of a rattlesnake and 50 times more than a cobra, with just one drop being enough to kill 100 adult humans.

A Bolivian fisherman is believed to have committed 'suicide by piranha' after deliberately jumping into a river infested with the flesh-eating fish in December 2011. Depressed Oscar Barbosa, 18, bled to death after jumping out of his canoe into the Yala River, where he suffered dozens of bites to the throat and face.

ELEPHANT

Elephantidae (family)
LIVES Africa and South Asia
EATS Grass, leaves, fruit, bark

Some like to think of an elephant as a friendly, sociable creature – but the reality is that over 500 people a year are horribly squashed to death by these giants.

Most elephant attacks are entirely random and without provocation. And with the huge beast – the world's largest land animal – weighing as much as 13 tonnes, and able to turn its tusks, trunk and feet into deadly weapons, it's always a very one-sided fight.

Many deaths in the wild are caused by young males which rampage through a village or charge at tourists on safari. When in a state of 'musth', an elephant can turn into an aggressive, sexually-motivated killing machine which can easily crush or impale anything and anyone that stands in its path.

TIME YOU'VE GOT LEFT: Seconds
THE LAST THING YOU'LL FEEL: There can't be anything scarier than seeing a herd of stampeding elephants galloping towards you – apart from a having a herd of stampeding elephants galloping over you. With each weighing as much as a double-decker bus, you can be sure there won't be much left of you by the time they're done.

CASSOWARY

Casuariidae (family)

LIVES Rainforests of Australia and Papua New Guinea

EATS Berries, plants

Wonder what kind of badass bird is capable of killing more than 20 people a year? Well, imagine an 80-kg psycho-chicken with kung-fu skills that put Bruce Lee to shame and you're nearly there.

The flightless cassowary is actually an extremely shy, secretive forest bird, but if harassed, the world's third tallest and second heaviest living bird turns into a fearless fighter.

The bird has an enormous, dagger-like claw on the second toe of each foot. When confronted, it will leap into the air and kick its enemy, kung-fu style, using the deadly claw to rip its victim's guts out. It can easily disembowel a man with it, and has been known to attack not only humans, but horses and cows too. The bird's powerful kick is mighty enough to rupture your internal organs.

TIME YOU'VE GOT LEFT: 2 minutes

THE LAST THING YOU'L FEEL: Whether your guts get ripped out or your internal organs explode inside of you, the effect will be the same: more than a little abdominal pain, quickly followed by massive blood loss and death.

DEATHSTALKER SCORPION

Leiurus quinquestriatus
LIVES North Africa, Middle East
EATS Crickets, small insects

Deathstalker scorpions have been around since before the dinosaurs, which means they've had 400 million years to perfect the art of killing.

No more than 4 in. long, what they lack in size they make up for in other ways, combining a fatal mixture of irritability, aggression and an extremely toxic venom capable of despatching a human in minutes. The scorpion is also capable of changing its colour to match its surroundings, meaning you might not even see it until it lands its deadly blow.

Strangely enough, though, the neurotoxins found in deathstalker venom have been studied by scientists looking for a treatment for brain cancer and diabetes.

TIME YOU'VE GOT LEFT: 10 minutes
THE LAST THING YOU'LL FEEL: The initial sting will fill your entire body with immense and unbearable pain. Then comes convulsions, breathing difficulties, paralysis, coma and death by respiratory failure.

MOSQUITO

Culicidae (family)
LIVES Tropical and subtropical regions
EATS Blood, nectar

Deceptively small and vulnerable, this bloodsucking pest is the world's undisputed deadliest animal because it carries and spreads one of the most dangerous diseases known to man: malaria.

Every year over 300 million people across Africa, South America and Asia are infected with the malaria parasite, which destroys blood cells and clogs the flow of blood. Most deaths occur in Africa where a child dies from the disease every 30 seconds.

Interestingly, it is just the female mosquito that is dangerous, as only she feeds on human blood to help her eggs develop – this is when the virus is passed on. The male mozzie, which feeds on nectar from flowers, is completely harmless.

TIME YOU'VE GOT LEFT: Sometimes days, sometimes weeks if untreated
THE LAST THING YOU'LL FEEL: As the malaria parasites invade your red blood cells they cause a flu-like illness with high fevers and shaking chills which, if not treated immediately, quickly leads to coma, kidney failure and death.

JAGUAR

Panthera onca

LIVES Amazon rainforest

EATS Large animals such as deer, capybara, dogs, foxes

The name 'jaguar' comes from the South American Indian word *yaguara*, which means 'a beast that kills its prey with one bound' – and there are few animals in the world that kill more quickly or efficiently.

Most big cats kill prey by going for the neck, holding it so tight their victim either chokes or has a stroke – the jaguar, however, simply sinks its long, sharp fangs into the victim's skull until it pierces the brain.

In fact, everything about the elegant, powerful jaguar has been designed with killing in mind. They can run faster than their prey, at speeds of up to 58 mph; they can climb higher and quicker, using their strong claws and agility to run up trees; and don't think you'll be safe by jumping into the nearest river – they are expert swimmers too.

TIME YOU'VE GOT LEFT: No time

THE LAST THING YOU'LL FEEL: Probably nothing, as the jaguar is so well camouflaged you probably won't even notice it creeping up on you, and so quick you'll be dead before you realise you've been pounced on.

SALTWATER CROCODILE

Crocodylus porosus
LIVES Northern Australia, eastern India, parts of south-east Asia
EATS Monkeys, kangaroos, buffalo, sharks, humans

The saltwater crocodile is one of the few animals that see humans as prey, to be hunted and eaten.

Weighing up to 157 stone (1,000 kg) – the same as 13 adult men – the ferocious reptile is an ambush hunter, which lies in wait for a victim before suddenly grabbing them and going into a 'death roll'. This consists of the crocodile holding its prey with its jaws, usually by the neck or a limb, dragging it into the water and spinning its entire body, which is usually enough to drown and dismember the victim.

The worst mass croc attack occurred on the night of February 19, 1945, when around a thousand Japanese soldiers were pinned down in a mangrove swamp near the Burmese mainland. For the ravenous saltwater crocodiles it was like an all-you-can-eat feast, and only 20 soldiers got out alive.

TIME YOU'VE GOT LEFT: Seconds
THE LAST THING YOU'LL FEEL: From the moment the croc's jaws snap shut on your body to the moment you meet your watery grave after being rolled around until your limbs are torn off is thankfully a matter of seconds.

SCREW-WORM MAGGOT

Cochliomyia hominivorax
LIVES Central and South America
EATS Flesh of open wounds of warm blooded animals

While all other maggots are perfectly happy munching on dead tissue, and most actually perform a valuable service by cleaning corpses of bacteria, the screw-worm likes nothing better than a big chunk of living – and, by preference, human – flesh.

It starts by 'screwing' itself into any cut, graze or scratch and then eats until there's nothing left. It also has poisonous saliva which promotes more infection in wounds, causing disgusting, foul-smelling pus.

The adult screw-worm – a type of blowfly with huge demonic red eyes – always tries to find an open wound to deposit her eggs, laying up to 500 at a time. And if she can't find an open wound she instead looks for any suitable orifice for her ravenous, man-eating offspring to bury into – normally the nose and ears.

TIME YOU'VE GOT LEFT: Hours

THE LAST THING YOU'LL FEEL: One can only imagine what it's like to feel your flesh being eaten from the inside out, or to have a bunch of hungry maggots munching away deep inside your ear canal. After that, the fever, chills, blood poisoning, respiratory failure and death will feel like a blessed release.

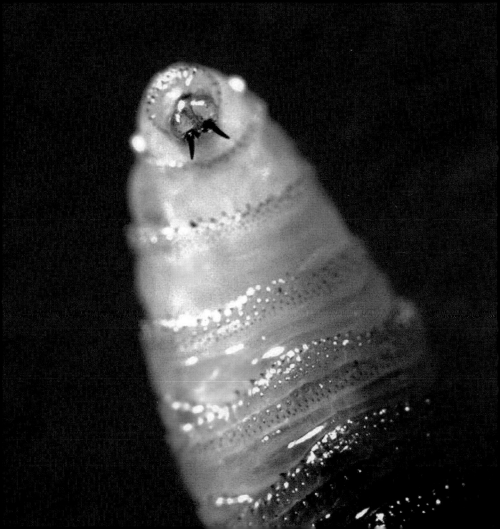

DEADLY ANIMAL FACTS

Don't assume you're safe from shark attacks just because you're swimming in a river miles away from the sea – the bull shark is one of the only sharks that can tolerate fresh water and has been known to attack swimmers as far as 100 miles inland.

A teenage girl gave her mother a horrific commentary by mobile phone as a brown bear and three cubs ate her alive in August 2011. Olga Moskalyova, 19, made three calls to her mum during the hour-long ordeal near Petropavlovsk in eastern Siberia.

STINGRAY

Myliobatoidei (suborder)
LIVES Coastal and subtropical waters around the world
EATS Molluscs, crustaceans, small fish

As the world found out in 2006 when 'Crocodile Hunter' Steve Irwin was stabbed in the heart by a stingray barb, in the wild this creature, which lives on the sandy ocean floor, doesn't like being messed with – and won't give any warning before launching a split-second attack with its 8-in. spear laced with venom.

Touch or step on a stingray by mistake and its tail will whip up in a reflex action, plunging its barbed stinger deep into your leg, arm, abdomen or chest. The venom causes swelling and excruciating pain, but if it then travels in the blood to the chest – or worse, if the barb has impaled the heart itself – death is just seconds away.

Although completely unprovoked attacks are unheard of, every year stingrays injure thousands of people, killing at least a dozen.

TIME YOU'VE GOT LEFT: 10 minutes
THE LAST THING YOU'LL FEEL: Extreme pain, dizziness, muscle cramps, seizures, irregular pulse, weakness and low blood pressure. As the venom enters the chest cavity the resulting tissue death will cause heart failure.

ASSASSIN BUG

Triatoma protracta
LIVES South and Central America
EATS Blood of mammals

This small, brown blood-sucker, also known as the 'kissing bug', carries the parasite that causes Chagas disease, a potentially deadly illness which results in life-threatening digestive disorders and chronic heart failure. Many victims become violently ill almost immediately after being bitten, waking up with swollen-shut eyes and blistered skin, vomiting and struggling to breathe.

Others don't show any signs for years, with the disease lurking in their blood only to surface twenty to thirty years after the initial bite. Once Chagas is diagnosed, two-thirds of people will have irreversible heart damage, including dilated cardiomyopathy, which causes heart rhythm abnormalities and may result in sudden death.

TIME YOU'VE GOT LEFT: Either days or years
THE LAST THING YOU'LL FEEL: At first Chagas disease causes fever, diarrhoea and vomiting. When at its acute stage, the illness plays havoc with the nervous system, digestive system and heart, with symptoms including damage to heart muscles, swallowing difficulties, neuritis, motor deficits, confusion, dementia and eventually death.

BLACK MAMBA

Dendroaspis polylepis
LIVES Savannahs of southern and eastern Africa
EATS Birds, small mammals

Africa's black mamba is not only the deadliest snake in the world, it is also the fastest, capable of reaching speeds in excess of 12 mph – that's faster than most people can run. Combine their terrifying speed with the fact they are nervous, highly aggressive and equipped with enough venom in just one fang to kill 40 men, it is easy to see why the mere mention of the legendary snake evokes fear.

When about to attack, the black mamba – which can reach up to 14 ft (4.3 m) long – stands up, raising up to two-thirds of its body off the ground, while opening its jet-black mouth wide and letting off a menacing hiss. The mamba strikes up to 12 times in a row, pumping more lethal venom into its victim with every blow. Without antivenom, the death rate from a black mamba bite is 100 per cent.

TIME YOU'VE GOT LEFT: 7–15 hours
THE LAST THING YOU'LL FEEL: At first, tunnel vision, sweating, excessive salivation and lack of muscle control in the mouth and tongue. Symptoms will quickly progress to nausea, shortness of breath, confusion, convulsions and paralysis, before death from suffocation due to paralysis of the muscles used for breathing.

GOLIATH TIGER FISH

Hydrocynus goliath
LIVES Congo River, west Africa
EATS Small fish, crustaceans, mammals

This ferocious freshwater fish grows up to 5 ft long and can be as heavy as 154 lb. Most terrifying of all, though, is the goliath fish's set of 32 protruding, dagger-like teeth which are similar in size and sharpness to those of a great white shark – and can be just as deadly. Locals say the tiger fish is the only fish that doesn't fear crocodiles, and sometimes even attacks and eats the smaller ones. Thanks to an ingenious contraption in its swim bladder – a small bone which connects to its ear and acts like an amplifier – the fish can hear and detect the slightest sound of a potential meal approaching.

The goliath tiger fish, like the piranha, tends to swim around in shoals that can reduce an animal, or man, of any size to a pile of bones in minutes.

TIME YOU'VE GOT LEFT: Minutes
THE LAST THING YOU'LL FEEL: Being eaten alive by a shoal of ravenous, man-sized fish each equipped with a set of sharks' teeth will make you wish you never went near the water.

GREAT WHITE SHARK

Carcharodon carcharias
LIVES Coastal and deep waters, particularly Australia and South Africa
EATS Seals, sea lions, fish

It's the ocean's ultimate predator: powerful, streamlined body, a mouth full of terrifyingly sharp, serrated teeth and super senses that can detect a single drop of blood from over a mile away.

A great white can grow up to 6 m long – the same as two saloon cars parked end to end – and can weigh as much as 3 tonnes. It attacks its prey by propelling itself through the water at speeds of up to 40 mph, before taking a single huge bite.

But despite its fearsome reputation, the great white doesn't actually prefer to eat humans. Experts believe that most great white attacks are test bites to see if the thing splashing about in the water is worth eating or not. The problem is, a quick nibble by a great white almost always means permanent disfigurement.

TIME YOU'VE GOT LEFT: Minutes
THE LAST THING YOU'LL FEEL: The first bite can take off a leg, arm, or worse, a huge chunk from your torso. If the shark comes back for more, it will bite again, this time with more strength, before dragging you underwater until you are dead, then ripping chunk after chunk of meat from you.

SLOW LORIS

Lorisidae (family)

LIVES South and South-east Asia

EATS Insects, small birds, reptiles, fruit, vegetation

Perhaps one of the cutest, cuddliest creatures on the planet, this slow-moving gooey-eyed furball – which loves being tickled – is just asking for you to pick it up. If you do, though, you might be in for a nasty surprise.

This primate, the most venomous mammal in the world, carries around its poison in a secret patch near its elbow, which the adult smears on its young to help keep them from being eaten in the wild. However, when provoked, the loris sucks a bit of the venom from the patch, swirls it around in its mouth, then administers a toxic bite.

If you have an allergic reaction to the toxin, you could be dead within minutes. Not so cute now, are they?

TIME YOU'VE GOT LEFT: Minutes

THE LAST THING YOU'LL FEEL: Itching and swelling spreads from the bite over the whole body and within minutes breathing becomes difficult as the throat closes. You'll begin to panic and feel a sense of impending doom as your blood pressure drops, before you collapse, lose consciousness and die.

LEOPARD SEAL

Hydrurga leptonyx

LIVES Antarctic

EATS Penguins, other sea birds, fish, smaller seals

So named because it is as agile, cunning and deadly in the water as a leopard is on land, the leopard seal will grab you unawares, eat you up, then play with whatever's left over. The seal – which has a head that makes it look almost reptilian – is the second largest species of seal in the world, weighing up to 92 stone, but can still swim so fast it can launch itself out of the water to grab an unsuspecting penguin, its favourite snack.

Bold, powerful and curious, the leopard seal has also been known to hunt people. In 1985, Scottish explorer Gareth Wood was bitten twice on the leg when a leopard seal tried to drag him off the ice and into the sea, and in 2003 a leopard seal dragged snorkelling biologist Kirsty Brown, from Cambridge, underwater to her death.

TIME YOU'VE GOT LEFT: 2 minutes

THE LAST THING YOU'LL FEEL: Being grabbed by a mouthful of 2-in.-long razor-sharp teeth will hurt, but it's being dragged down into the icy Antarctic waters that will finish you off.

DEADLY ANIMAL FACTS

The Komodo dragon has shark-like teeth and a poisonous saliva which contains 80 strains of bacteria – meaning just one bite can kill you within hours. The 3-m-long lizard will lie in wait before pouncing on its victims, then retreat until septicaemia sets in and its prey dies. Thankfully, though, they only need to eat once a month.

A man died of internal haemorrhaging after he was butted in the stomach by a dolphin near a beach in São Paulo, Brazil in December 1994. It is thought the wild resident dolphin, known for his friendliness towards women swimmers, saw the man as a romantic competitor.

NORTHERN SHORT-TAILED SHREW

Blarina brevicauda
LIVES USA and southern Canada
EATS Earthworms, insects, snails, mice, frogs, salamanders

Despite looking like a timid, harmless creature that would scarper in fright at the slightest rustling of leaves, this tiny rodent is a deadly predator known for attacking animals much larger than itself, including snakes, frogs, mice, and even humans.

The shrew's secret weapon is its saliva, which contains a poison that acts on the nerves of its victims, slowing down its breathing and heart rate until it is effectively paralysed. Humans too, aren't immune from the shrew's toxic bite, which causes blistering and agonising pain for weeks. Those unlucky enough to suffer an allergic reaction to the powerful venom will suffer an anaphylactic shock, which often results in death.

TIME YOU'VE GOT LEFT: 2 hours
THE LAST THING YOU'LL FEEL: Burning pain and blistering at the site of the wound, followed by an itchy rash spreading over the body, swelling of the face and difficulty breathing as the throat closes. Lack of oxygen causes collapse, unconsciousness and death.

PUFFERFISH

Tetraodontidae (family)
LIVES Tropical parts of Atlantic, Indian and Pacific Oceans
EATS Crabs, clams, snails, oysters

Normally small and unassuming, the puffer fish can blow itself up to resemble a spiky balloon in order to frighten away any predators looking for a snack. But that's not the reason why it's one of the most feared fish in the ocean – it is filled with an extremely powerful poison, the tiniest drop of which will paralyse and kill you.

The puffer fish is considered the second most poisonous vertebrate on the planet, so fisherman who catch them use special thick gloves to handle them. Still, it doesn't stop extreme risk-takers enjoying the puffer fish sushi crafted by master sushi chefs, which is known to give a pleasant tingling sensation in the mouth if prepared correctly. When not prepared correctly, however, the unfortunate diner is paralysed almost instantly and of more than 200 people poisoned every year, half don't live to tell the tale.

TIME YOU'VE GOT LEFT: 24 hours
THE LAST THING YOU'LL FEEL: Tingling of the mouth, vomiting, dizziness, then total paralysis, although you will remain entirely conscious throughout. Eventually the venom paralyses the diaphragm, causing suffocation and death.

SYDNEY FUNNEL-WEB SPIDER

Atrax robustus
LIVES Eastern and southern Australia
EATS Beetles, cockroaches

This 5-cm-long spider is one of the world's most aggressive arachnids, and will rear up and bite you just as soon as look at you. Easily annoyed – especially when you happen to disturb a nest it's made in your clothes drawer – the funnel-web rears up on its hind legs, aggressively exposing its massive fangs, which are strong enough to penetrate even a finger nail. One drop of the spider's venom is enough to kill 225 mice or dispatch an adult human in just over half an hour.

Perhaps the most frightening thing about the funnel-web, however, is that it prefers to make its home in people's houses, and often decides to settle down in cosy places like laundry baskets, wardrobes, sleeping bags and shoes.

TIME YOU'VE GOT LEFT: 40 minutes
THE LAST THING YOU'LL FEEL: After the painful bite, tingling around the lips, twitching of the tongue, then profuse salivation, sweating, muscle spasms, vomiting, convulsions, breathlessness, coma and death.

PHOTO CREDITS

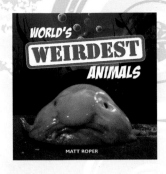

World's Weirdest Animals
Matt Roper

ISBN: 978 1 84024 749 7   Hardback   £6.99

Whales that look like unicorns, lizards that squirt jets of blood from their eyes, naked rats that can sprint backwards... It seems as though some creatures have been put on this earth just to make us laugh.

From the harmless but hilarious to the truly frightening and deadly, the animals in this book are guaranteed to keep you amazed, enthralled and extremely amused.

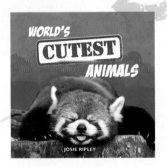

World's Cutest Animals
Josie Ripley

ISBN: 978 1 84953 304 1   Hardback   £6.99

Pocket-sized pikas, fuzzy finger-monkeys and cuddly koalas are just a few of the cute and loveable creatures you'll find in this book.

From the teeniest to the fluffiest, this collection of the world's cutest animals contains lavish photographs, interesting facts and 'snuggle ratings' for Nature's most adorable creatures – so sweet you'll want one of each!

If you're interested in finding out more about our gift books,
follow us on Twitter: **@Summersdale**

www.summersdale.com